Robin Hood

Written by Alice Hemming

Illustrated by Davide Ortu

Collins

Meet Robin Hood.

3

The rich Sheriff raids and loots.

But Robin Hood puts it right.

The Sheriff looks livid!

Ten men seems unfair ...

but Robin meets his men.

9

Now it is ten fools versus six archers.

They run off to report back.

Fight for fairness

After reading

Letters and Sounds: Phase 3

Word count: 59

Focus phonemes: /ai/ /ee/ /igh/ /oo/ /oo/ /ar/ /or/ /ow/ /air/ /er/

Common exception words: I, the, put(s), they, to, we

Curriculum links: Personal, social and emotional education

Early learning goals: Reading: read and understand simple sentences, use phonic knowledge to decode regular words and read them aloud accurately; Understanding: answer "how" and "why" questions about their experiences and in response to stories or events; Personal, social and emotional development: talk about their own and others' behaviour, and its consequences, and know that some behaviour is unacceptable

Developing fluency

- Your child may enjoy hearing you read the book.
- You could be the "narrator" by reading the main text at the top of the page and your child could read the speech bubbles, acting out the parts of the characters in the story.

Phonic practice

- Practise reading words with more than one syllable together. Look at the word **fairness** on page 3. Say the word and clap each syllable as you do. Ask your child to sound talk and blend the letter sounds in the first syllable: f/air. Now ask them to do the same with the second syllable: n/e/ss. Say both syllables: fairness.
- Do the same with the words **livid** and **versus**.

Extending vocabulary

- Ask your child to find the odd one out in each of the follow sets of words. You may wish to read them to your child.

livid	happy	angry	*(happy)*
run	loot	steal	*(run)*
versus	against	together	*(together)*